INVESTIGATING GHOSTS IN HOTELS

Matilda Snowden

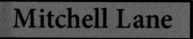

PUBLISHERS

mitchelllane.com

2001 SW 31st Avenue
Hallandale, FL 33009

First Edition, 2021.
Author: Matilda Snowden
Designer: Ed Morgan
Editor: Joyce Markovics

Series: Investigating Ghosts!
Title: Investigating Ghosts in Hotels / by Matilda Snowden

Hallandale, FL : Mitchell Lane Publishers, [2021]

Library bound ISBN: 978-1-68020-633-3
eBook ISBN: 978-1-68020-634-0

CONTENTS

Words in **bold** can be found in the Glossary.

HAUNTED HOTELS

At the end of a long driveway sits an abandoned hotel. Heavy rain hammers the roof. A **paranormal** investigator enters the lobby. The hotel is empty except for some old furniture. He climbs a grand staircase to the second floor. There's a humming sound coming from room 207. The ghost hunter flips on his digital recorder as he swings the door open. Something scurries into the

corner of the room. "Who's there?" he asks.
Just then, a shadow comes into view. It
creeps around the corner, growing larger as it
moves. Suddenly, the door slams shut behind
the ghost hunter.

There are hundreds of hotels around the country where unexplainable things happen. It's said that many of these places have guests that never want to leave—even after death. Why is it that so many old hotels are believed to have resident spirits? Could this have anything to do with troubling events from the past? There is a devoted group who want to find out. These ghost hunters, also known as paranormal investigators, gather evidence to prove that ghosts are real.

Turn the page to read chilling stories about reportedly haunted hotels. And follow teams of paranormal investigators who seek to uncover the truth about ghosts.

INTERESTING FACT

Ghosts are said to be the spirits or souls of dead people. Others believe that ghosts are visual memories from the past that are somehow stuck in another time.

THE STANLEY HOTEL

Estes Park, Colorado

Not far from the Rocky Mountains is the **stately** Stanley Hotel. Businessman Freelan O. Stanley built the 140-room hotel in 1909. His wife, Flora, is said to have played the piano for hotel guests. Over the years, many well-known people stayed at the hotel, including a U.S. president and a survivor of the Titanic. The Stanley is also famous for its darker history. Guests have reported seeing Mr. Stanley's ghost in the lobby and hearing **phantom** piano music.

More recently, the police were called after a guest started screaming for no obvious reason. Hotel workers suspect she saw a ghost. In 2006, paranormal investigators Jason Hawes and Grant Wilson went to the hotel to see for themselves if it's truly haunted.

INTERESTING FACT

The Stanley Hotel is famously featured in the horror movie *The Shining*. The movie is based on author Stephen King's book about a father who loses his mind in a haunted hotel.

Jason and Grant, along with their team, spent two nights at the Stanley Hotel. One of those nights was in room 401. This is where a guest had recently seen a ghostly figure disappear into the closet. When Jason went to bed, he heard voices and the sound of the closet door opening and closing. He sprang up to check the closet. It was empty. He soon noticed that the glass of water beside his bed had suddenly broken. "It had simply cracked . . . as if pressure had expanded it from the inside," Jason remembers. Exhausted, he drifted back to sleep. He awoke again to banging in the closet "like there was a party in there." Yet when Jason looked inside, it was empty.

INTERESTING FACT

Jason had left a digital video camera on in room 401 as he slept. Later, when he reviewed the footage, he saw the closet door close and lock by itself!

Meanwhile, Grant was having his own paranormal experience in another room. When he pulled the window drapes closed, they opened on their own— and not just a little. "They opened all the way," Grant said. After closing the drapes for the third time, he went to bed. Then Grant heard "the sound of the drapes hissing along their track." They had opened all the way again! "It seemed there was an intelligence behind the phenomenon," Grant said.

The next day, Grant and another team member visited room 1302. They felt a presence and asked if anyone else was in the room. No response. Then Grant placed his digital video recorder on a table in the room. Out of nowhere, the table lifted up and slammed down by itself. "My heart was pounding so hard," said Grant. "I've been through a lot of shocks in the course of my ghost-hunting career, but none more unexpected than the table." Afterwards, both Jason and Grant concluded that the Stanley Hotel is haunted.

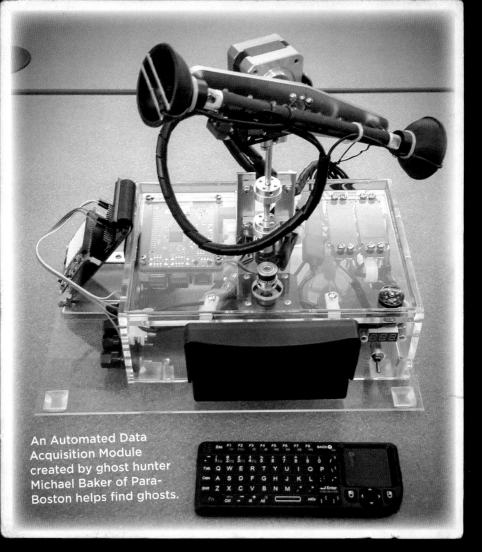

An Automated Data Acquisition Module created by ghost hunter Michael Baker of Para-Boston helps find ghosts.

INTERESTING FACT

Ghost hunters use a lot of different equipment during their investigations. The tools include digital recorders, thermal imaging tools, and various meters.

HOTEL AIKEN

Aiken, South Carolina

Built in 1898, Hotel Aiken is the topic of many haunted tales. It's said that spirits dwell in the building and unexplained noises ring out in the night. Supposedly, the ghostly activity centers on room 225. Hotel workers claim that nearly all the guests who check into that room asked to be moved to another one. What explains this? Ghost Hunter Stephen David Lancaster II and another investigator traveled to the hotel to find out.

Hotel Aiken, originally the Commercial Hotel, is reported to have the oldest working elevator in the southeast.

One evening while walking down a hallway in Hotel Aiken, Stephen began feeling dizzy for no obvious reason. At that point, his EMF meter picked up a strange signal, which increased only when he moved. "At this point we were basically tracking a moving electromagnetic field down the hallway," Stephen said.

INTERESTING FACT

EMF meters can pick up changes in electromagnetic fields. Ghost hunters believe that some spirits are made of energy, and EMF meters can help determine if a ghost is present.

The EMF meter led Stephen and his partner to a door. "It was at this moment that both myself and the other investigator heard a very faint female moan," Stephen said. Seconds later, they heard a louder moan. Then the EMF meter stopped picking up a signal. They left the room and headed back down the hallway. Once again, the meter picked up a strong signal—this time in another room on a bed. Stephen noticed it was cold in the room and used a digital thermometer to take the temperature. It was 11 degrees cooler just above the bed.

INTERESTING FACT

Ghost hunters believe that temperature changes can indicate a paranormal presence.

Suddenly, the TV in the room turned on by itself! "The volume was completely up and the channel display was nothing but loud white noise," said Stephen. He turned off the TV, and, seconds later, it turned back on by itself. "There was no rational explanation as to how this television was powering on without human intervention," Stephen said. Was a spirit responsible for turning the TV on?

Stephen and his partner made their way to the infamous room 225. A wave of nausea swept over Stephen. The temperature in the room was the coldest in the hotel. Even after opening the windows to the warm air outside, the room remained cold. Faint music started playing. Stephen felt sicker—and the EMF meter spiked to one of its highest levels. He wondered where the music was coming from. Then all the activity stopped. "The significant cold of the room and the low music on top of the electromagnetic field reads make the room quite an oddity," said Stephen. He hopes to return to the hotel in the future to investigate "the strange phenomena of room 225."

A ghost hunter uses an EMF meter.

INTERESTING FACT

Some ghost hunters are known as "sensitives." A sensitive can see or feel things in the paranormal realm. On occasion, a sensitive will feel ill in the presence of a spirit or other ghostly entity.

CHAPTER

FOUR

THE CRESCENT HOTEL

Eureka Springs, Arkansas

"I don't often find myself saying this about a place, but the Crescent Hotel is haunted," said ghost hunter Jason Hawes. Called America's most haunted hotel, the Crescent has a long, creepy past. It was built in 1886 as a hotel and spa. Norman G. Baker purchased the property in 1937. Baker, who claimed to be able to cure cancer, turned the building into a hospital and house of horrors. His so-called "cures" were **barbaric.**

For one treatment, Baker drilled holes in a patient's skull and filled them with mashed seeds and other strange things. Nearly all of Baker's patients died from their illnesses—or from his treatments. Most of his surgeries were performed in the hotel's basement. When ghost hunters Jason Hawes and Grant Wilson went there, they found something "incredible."

INTERESTING FACT

Norman Baker kept some of his dead patients' body parts in jars in the basement of the hotel. He was eventually sent to prison for his crimes.

Soon after arriving at the Crescent Hotel, Jason, Grant, and their team went to the basement to investigate. An old autopsy table reminded them that Baker once used the area as a morgue. In the back of the room, Grant saw a row of numbered lockers—and then a full-body apparition! It was a figure of a man in a hat with the numeral 2 on his sleeve. The numeral was "burning a bright, fiery red." Amazingly, the apparition was caught on camera. Before celebrating, Jason and Grant made sure there wasn't another explanation for the sighting. An important part of their work is debunking claims of paranormal activity. They wondered if the figure was a reflection of some kind. After a lot of careful work, they couldn't disprove the footage and what Grant had seen. It was "the Holy Grail of the ghost-hunting field," said Jason. They were left wondering—was the figure Norman Baker?

INTERESTING FACT

EVPs of many distressed voices have been recorded at the Crescent Hotel. EVP stands for "electronic voice phenomena." Ghost hunters believe that some audio devices can capture supernatural sounds or ghostly voices known as EVPs.

CHAPTER
FIVE

HOTEL MONTELEONE

New Orleans, Louisiana

Doors that open and close on their own, an elevator that stops on the wrong floor, and full-body apparitions are just a few of the ghostly goings-on at the Hotel Monteleone. Located in downtown New Orleans, the hotel opened its doors in 1886. The graceful building stands ten stories tall and has 600 guest rooms. One of the hotel's most haunted tales involves a young boy named Maurice Begere.

In the late 1800s, the well-to-do Begere family stayed on the 14th floor of the Hotel Monteleone with their young son, Maurice. One night, the parents went to the opera and left Maurice in the hotel with a nanny. While they were away, Maurice became very ill with a high fever. When the Begeres returned to the hotel, they were shocked to find their son was dead.

INTERESTING FACT

Hotel Monteleone is said to be haunted by William "Red" Wildemere. Red was a former employee who died in the hotel. He's said to have died of natural causes.

After that tragic day, the Begeres returned to the hotel every year on the anniversary of Maurice's death. They hoped to make contact with his ghost. One year, it's said that little Maurice appeared to his mother. According to the story, the apparition said: "Mommy, don't cry. I'm fine."

To this day, hotel guests report seeing a child ghost on the 14th floor. "I was just relaxing in bed one morning when I looked up to see a young boy, about three years old, walk by the foot of my bed," said Phyllis Paulsen, a frequent guest at the hotel. "It didn't take me long to realize that I had seen a ghost."

In 2003, members of the International Society of Paranormal Research visited the hotel. They claimed to contact over a dozen "earthbound entities." Is the hotel a hotbed of supernatural forces— or is there another explanation?

Ghost-Hunting Tools

Here are some basic ghost-hunting tools. Many household items can be used to track and gather evidence of possible ghosts.

- Pen and paper to record your findings

- A flashlight with extra batteries

- A camera with a clean lens. Sometimes, the "**orbs**" that some people capture on film are actually dust particles on the lens.

- A cell phone to use in case of an emergency and to keep track of time

- A camcorder or digital video recorder to capture images of spirits or any other paranormal activity

- A digital audio recorder to capture ghostly sounds or EVPs

- A digital thermometer to pick up temperature changes

More experienced ghost hunters use thermal imaging tools to locate hot and cold spots, as well as special meters to pick up energy fields. These include EMF (electromagnetic field) and RF (radio frequency) meters.

FIND OUT MORE

BOOKS

Gardner Walsh, Liza. *Ghost Hunter's Handbook: Supernatural Explorations for Kids*. Lanham, Maryland: Down East Publishing, 2016.

Loh-Hagan, Virginia. *Odd Jobs: Ghost Hunter*. Ann Arbor, Michigan: Cherry Lake Publishing, 2016.

Parvis, Sarah. *Haunted Hotels*. New York: Bearport Publishing, 2008.

WEBSITES

American Hauntings
https://www.americanhauntingsink.com

American Paranormal Investigations
https://www.ap-investigations.com

The Atlantic Paranormal Society
http://the-atlantic-paranormal-society.com

Ghost Research Society
http://www.ghostresearch.org

Paranormal Inc.
http://www.paranormalincorporated.com

The Parapsychological Association
https://www.parapsych.org

WORKS CONSULTED

Granato, Sherri. *Haunted America & Other Paranormal Travels*. Bloomington, Indiana: LifeRich Publishing, 2015.

Hawes, Jason, and Grant Wilson. *Ghost Files*. New York: Gallery Books, 2011.

Lancaster II, Stephen David. *Paranormal Investigator: True Accounts of the Paranormal*. Scotts Valley, California: CreateSpace, 2010.

Newman, Rich. *Ghost Hunting for Beginners: Everything You Need to Know to Get Started*. Woodbury, Minnesota: Llewellyn Publications, 2018.

Rule, Leslie. *When the Ghost Screams: True Stories of Victims Who Haunt*. Kansas City, Missouri: Andrews McMeel Publishing, 2006.

Taylor, Troy. *The Ghost Hunters Guidebook: The Essential Guide to Investigating Ghosts & Hauntings*. Alton, Illinois: Whitechapel Productions Press, 2004.

ON THE INTERNET

https://www.aikenstandard.com/news/today-show-features-inn-s-hauntings/article_686d2f04-1763-50b9-838f-47c3c46df6bd.html

https://www.atlasobscura.com/places/the-1886-crescent-hotel-and-spa-eureka-springs-arkansas

https://crescent-hotel.com/blog/ghostly-legend-at-americas-most-haunted-hotel-enhanced-in-2019/

https://crescent-hotel.com/history.shtml

https://www.historichotels.org/hotels-resorts/hotel-monteleone/history.php

https://hotelmonteleone.com/blog/haunted-tale-maurice-begere/

http://www.southcoastparanormalsociety.com/South_Coast_Paranormal_Society/Hotel-Aiken-Case.html

https://www.stanleyhotel.com/about.html

GLOSSARY

apparition
A ghost or ghostlike image

autopsy
An examination that occurs after a person dies to discover the cause of death

barbaric
Cruel or brutal

debunking
Proving something to be untrue

devoted
Very loyal

distressed
Suffering from anxiety, sorrow, or pain

electromagnetic field
A field of energy around a magnetic material or moving electric charge

entity
A thing with an independent existence

evidence
Information and facts that help prove something

infamous
Well-known for something bad

intervention
The act of getting involved in something to prevent or change a result

morgue
A place where dead bodies are kept

nausea
Feeling sick to the stomach

orbs
Glowing spheres

paranormal
Relating to events not able to be scientifically explained

phantom
Belonging to a ghost or spirit

phenomenon
An occurrence that one can sense

presence
A person or thing that exists but is not seen

rational
Based on reason or logic

realm
The region or domain within which anything occurs

spirits
Supernatural beings such as ghosts

stately
Impressive in appearance, manner, or size

supernatural
Beyond scientific understanding

thermal
Relating to heat

tragic
Causing extreme sadness

visual
Relating to seeing or sight

INDEX

ABOUT THE AUTHOR

Matilda Snowden loves all things old and cobwebby and visiting historic buildings. Her favorite thing about being an author is talking with children about how to tell a spooky story.